**NEIL A. KJOS**
PIANO LIBRARY

**PREPARATORY LEVEL**

SELECTED & ARRANGED BY

# Barbara Becker

## Music for Christmas

## FIRST SCENES FROM CHRISTMAS

## Contents

ISBN 0-8497-9654-7

# Jolly Old St. Nicholas

Traditional Carol
Arranged by Barbara Becker

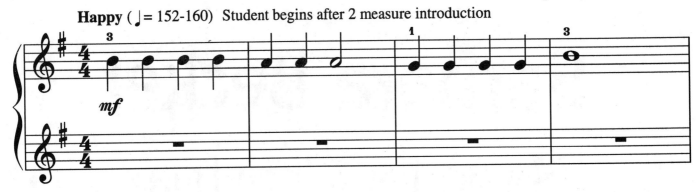

\* Optional duet continues for 3 measures.

© 1997 Neil A. Kjos Music Company

# I Saw Three Ships

Traditional English Carol
Arranged by Barbara Becker

**Smoothly** (♩ = 140)
Student begins after 7 measure introduction

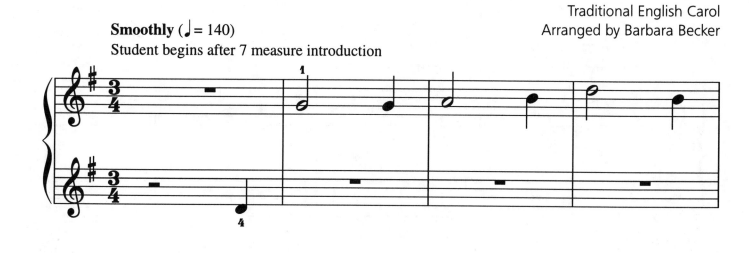

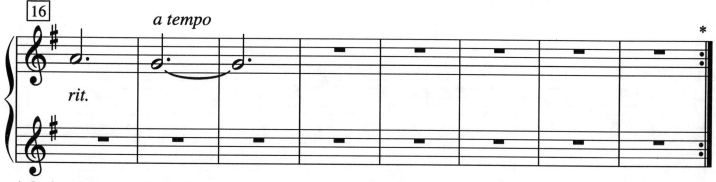

*a tempo*

*rit.*

\* Optional duet continues for 3 measures.

WP550

# Jingle Bells

John Pierpont
Arranged by Barbara Becker

**Moderato** ( ♩ = 180)
Student begins after 4 measure introduction

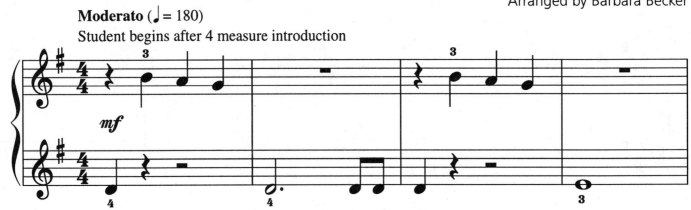

*poco rit.*

*a tempo*

move ③ to C

*rit.*

© 1997 Neil A. Kjos Music Company

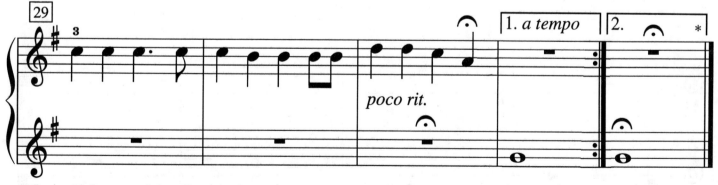

* Optional duet continues for 4 measures.

# Bring a Torch, Jeannette Isabella

Traditional French Carol
Arranged by Barbara Becker

**Majestic** (♩ = 180)
Student begins after 4 measure introduction

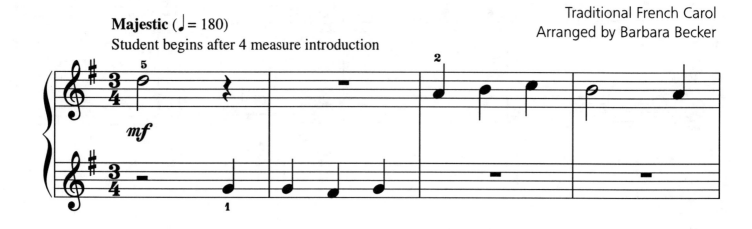

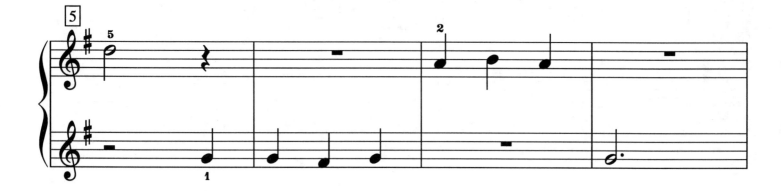

© 1997 Neil A. Kjos Music Company

**NEIL A. KJOS**
PIANO LIBRARY

**TEACHER DUET BOOK**
**FOR THE PREPARATORY LEVEL**

SELECTED & ARRANGED BY

# Barbara Becker

## Music for Christmas

## FIRST SCENES FROM CHRISTMAS

## Contents

ISBN 0-8497-9654-7

# Jolly Old St. Nicholas

Traditional Carol
Arranged by Barbara Becker

**Teacher Duet** (Student plays 1 octave higher)

**Happy** ( ♩ = 152-160)

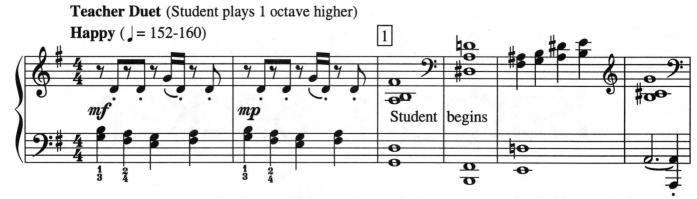

\* Measure numbers correspond with measures in student part.

© 1997 Neil A. Kjos Music Company

# I Saw Three Ships

Traditional English Carol
Arranged by Barbara Becker

* Measure numbers correspond with measures in student part.

WP550-B

# Jingle Bells

John Pierpont
Arranged by Barbara Becker

**Teacher Duet** (Student plays 1 octave higher)
**Moderato** ( ♩ = 90)
**Intro.**

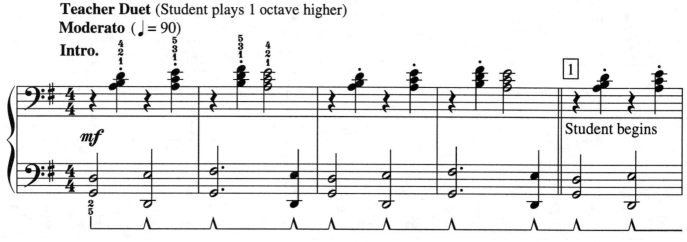

_pedal simile_

\* Measure numbers correspond with measure numbers in the student part.

WP550-B

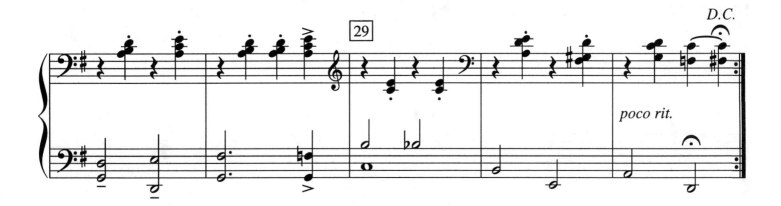

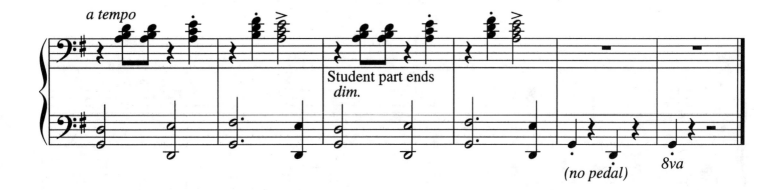

# Bring a Torch, Jeannette Isabella

Traditional French Carol
Arranged by Barbara Becker

**Teacher Duet** (Student plays 1 octave higher or as written)
**Majestic** (♩ = 180)

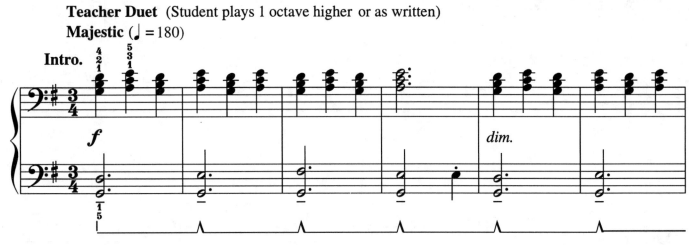

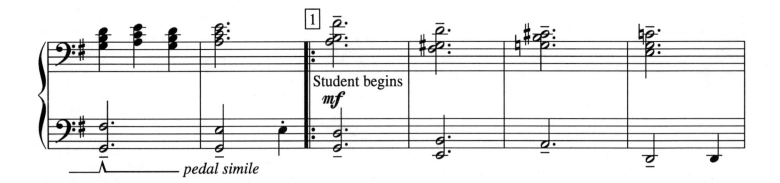

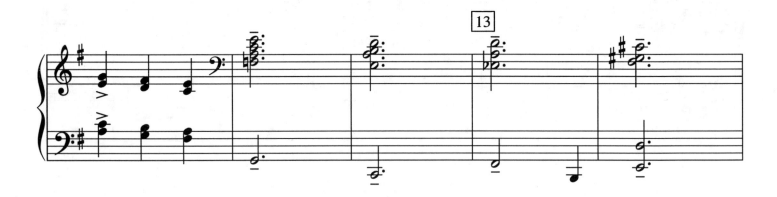

WP550-B

© 1997 Neil A. Kjos Music Company

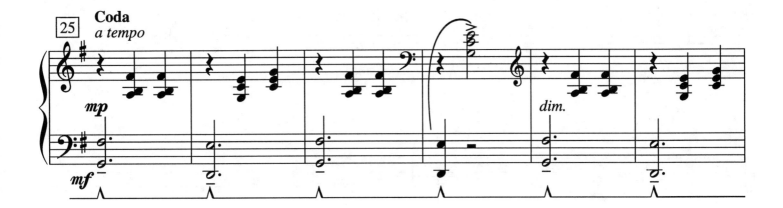

* optional repeat

# The First Noel

Traditional English Carol
Arranged by Barbara Becker

**Teacher Duet** (Student plays 1 octave higher)

**Dolce** (♩ = 120)

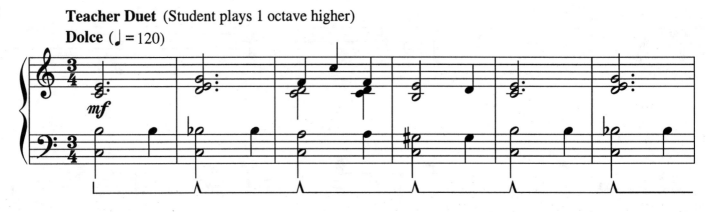

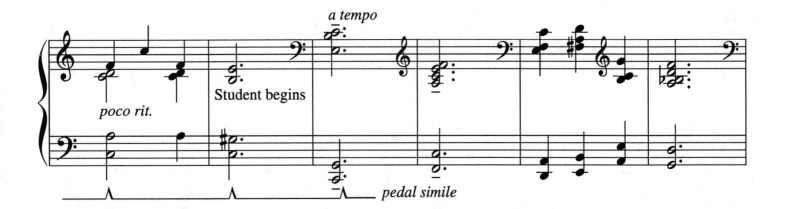

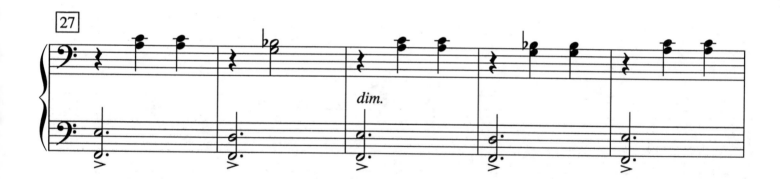

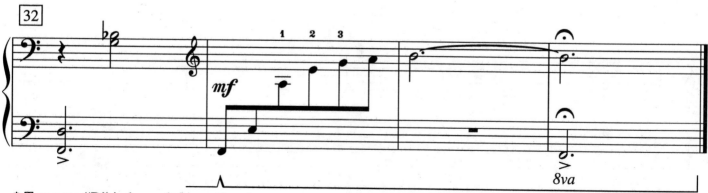

* Top note "D" in bass clef is optional.

# Up on the Housetop

Benjamin R. Hanby
Arranged by Barbara Becker

**Teacher Duet** (Student plays 1 octave higher)
**Allegro** ( ♩ = 130)
**Intro.**

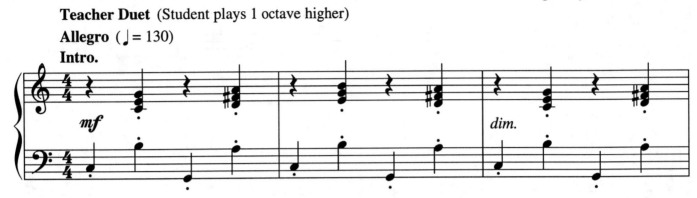

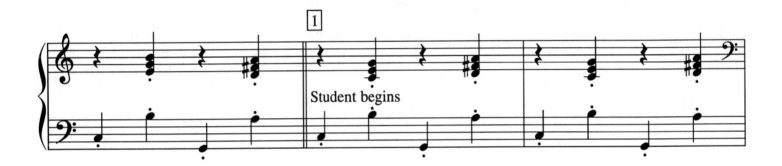

\* Measure numbers correspond with measure numbers in the student part.

WP550-B

# Good King Wenceslas

Traditional English Carol
Arranged by Barbara Becker

**Teacher Duet** (Student plays 1 octave higher)
**Allegro** ( ♩ = 80)
**Intro.**

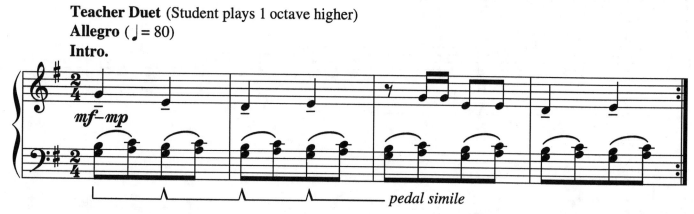

\* Measure numbers correspond with measure numbers in the student part.

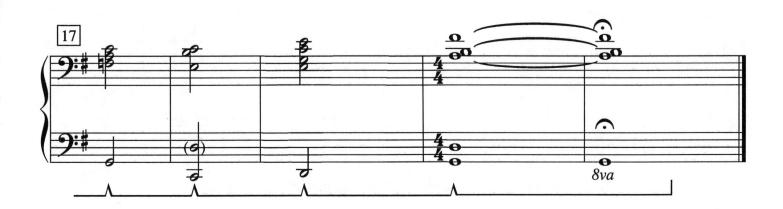

# Angels We Have Heard on High

**Teacher Duet** (Student plays 1 octave higher or as written.)
**Sweetly** ( ♩ = 110-120)
**Intro.**

Traditional English Carol
Arranged by Barbara Becker

*with pedal*

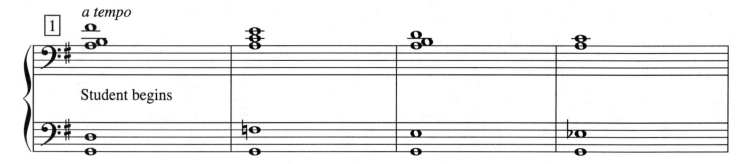

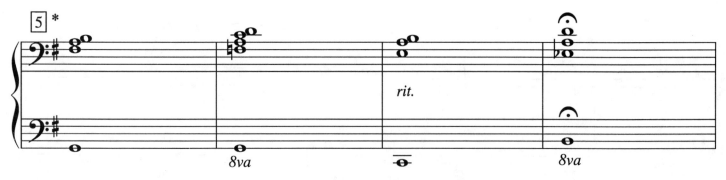

\* Measure numbers correspond with measure numbers in the student part.

# Silent Night

Franz Gruber
Arranged by Barbara Becker

**Teacher Duet** (Student plays 1 octave higher)
**Warmly** (♩. = 50)
**Intro.**

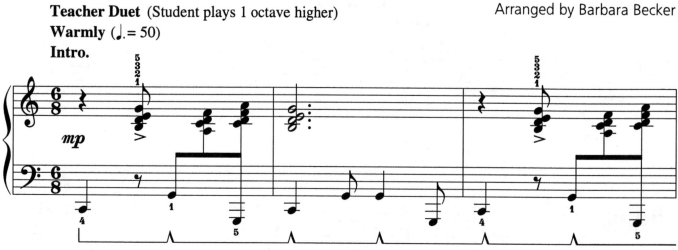

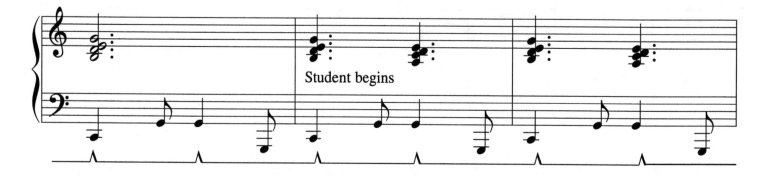

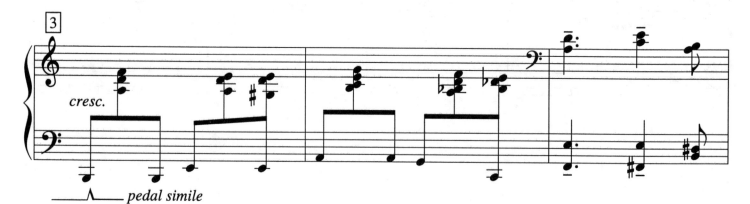

\* Measure numbers correspond with measure numbers in the student part.

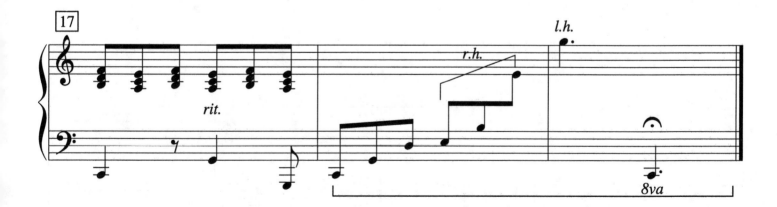

# We Wish You a Merry Christmas

Traditional English Carol
Arranged by Barbara Becker

**Teacher Duet** (Student plays 1 octave higher)
**Joyfully** ( ♩ = 130)
**Intro.**

*Measure numbers correspond with measure numbers in the student part.

© 1997 Neil A. Kjos Music Company

# The Neil A. Kjos Piano Library

The **Neil A. Kjos Piano Library** is a comprehensive series of piano music in a wide variety of musical styles. The library is divided into eleven levels and will provide students with a complete performance experience in both solo and ensemble music. Teachers will find the carefully graded levels appropriate when choosing repertoire for evaluations, auditions, festivals, and examinations. Included in the **Neil A. Kjos Piano Library**:

### Preparatory Level - Level Ten

Fundamentals of Piano Theory
Piano Repertoire: Baroque & Classical
Piano Repertoire: Romantic & 20th Century
Piano Repertoire: Etudes
Music of the 21st Century
New Age Piano
Jazz Piano
One Piano Four Hands
Music for Christmas

# Preface

**Music for Christmas** from the **Neil A. Kjos Piano Library** gives piano students of all ages and performance abilities an opportunity to perform unique concert arrangements of well-known sacred and secular Christmas carols. Each volume contains an ample selection of music in a variety of tempos, keys and styles, many with lush reharmonizations. The carefully graded compositions ensure steady and thorough progress as pianists advance in their study of keyboard literature. These motivational solos may be assigned for study and performance with any method or course of study.

**Coda**
*a tempo*

* optional repeat

# The First Noel

Traditional English Carol
Arranged by Barbara Becker

**Dolce** (♩ = 120)
Student begins after 7 measure introduction

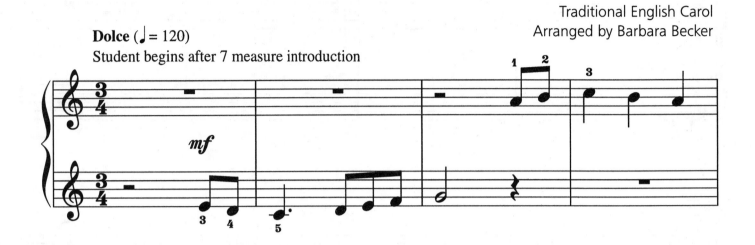

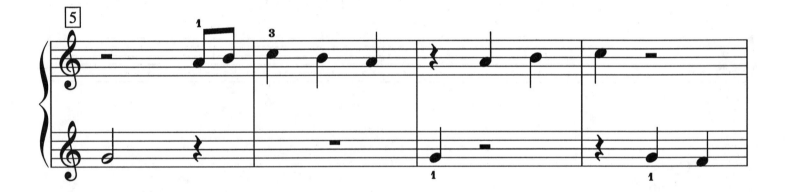

© 1997 Neil A. Kjos Music Company

*rit. when played as a duet*

*a tempo*

Coda to be played
with duet

*dim.*

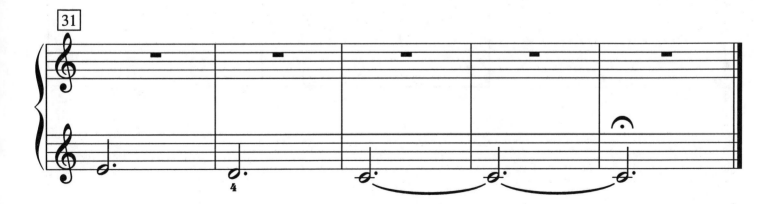

# Up on the Housetop

Benjamin R. Hanby
Arranged by Barbara Becker

**Allegro** (♩ = 130)
Student begins after 4 measure introduction

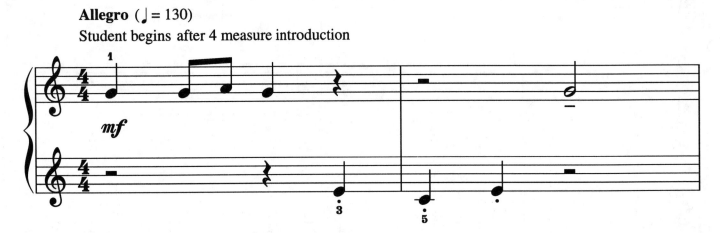

© 1997 Neil A. Kjos Music Company

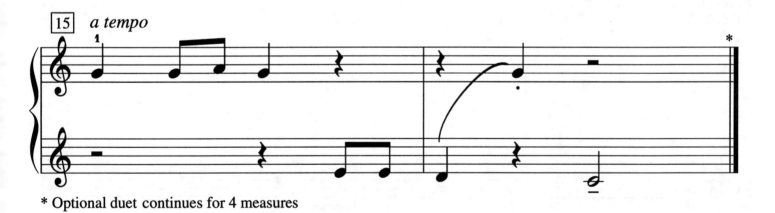

* Optional duet continues for 4 measures

# Good King Wenceslas

Traditional English Carol
Arranged by Barbara Becker

**Allegro** ( ♩ = 80)
Student begins after 8 measure introduction

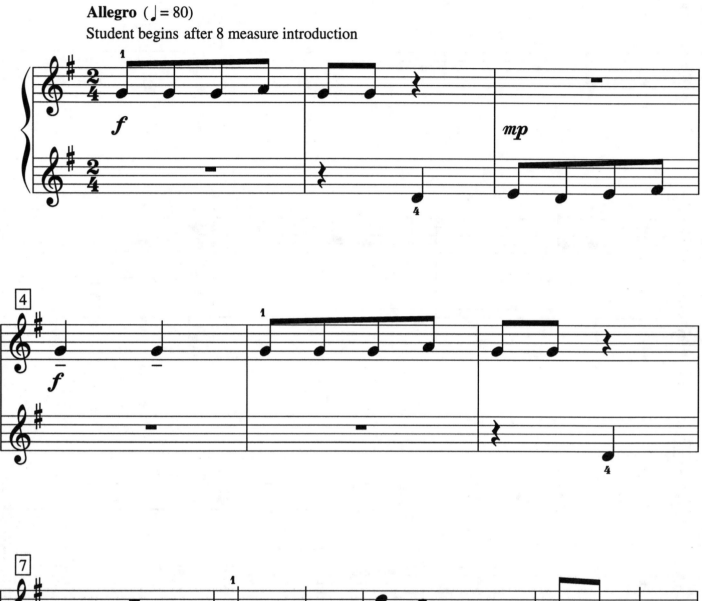

© 1997 Neil A. Kjos Music Company

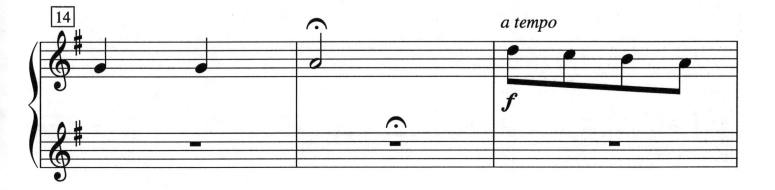

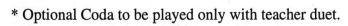

\* Optional Coda to be played only with teacher duet.

# Angels We Have Heard on High

Traditional English Carol
Arranged by Barbara Becker

**Sweetly** ( ♩ = 110-120)
Student begins after 8 measure introduction

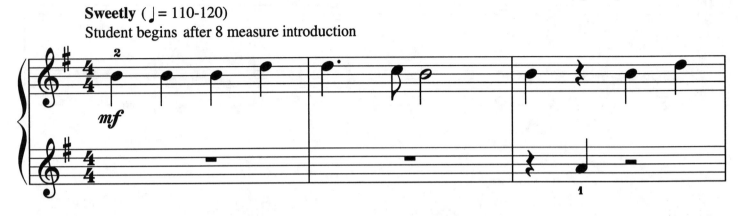

* Optional duet continues for 3 measures.

# Silent Night

Franz Gruber
Arranged by Barbara Becker

**Warmly** (♩.= 50)
Student begins after 4 measure introduction

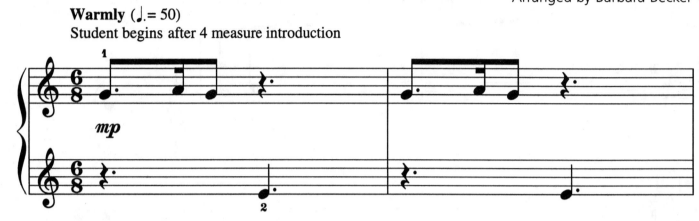

© 1997 Neil A. Kjos Music Company

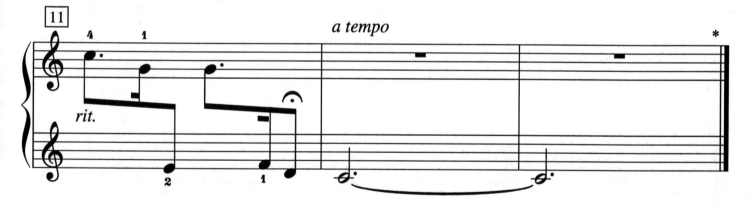

* Optional duet continues for 6 measures.

# We Wish You a Merry Christmas

Traditional English Carol
Arranged by Barbara Becker

**Joyfully** ( ♩ = 130)
Student begins after 7 measure introduction

*Quarter note may be substituted for eighth notes in measures 7, 14, and 15.

© 1997 Neil A. Kjos Music Company

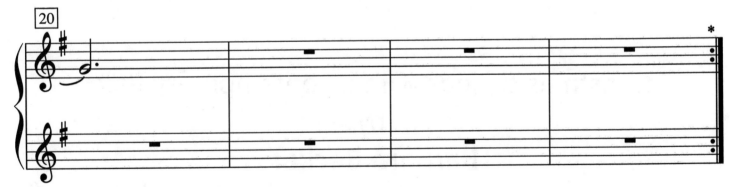

* Optional duet continues for 4 measures.

# Music for Christmas

## Exciting piano collections from
## THE NEIL A. KJOS PIANO LIBRARY

**First Scenes From Christmas** Preparatory Level by Barbara Becker

**Christmas Enchantments** Level One by Jeanine Yeager

**Second Scenes From Christmas** Level Two by Barbara Becker

**Forever Christmas** Level Four by Eugénie R. Rocherolle

**Jazz Impressions of Christmas** Level Five by Larry Minsky

**A Joyful Christmas** Level Six by Ann Buys

**Christmas Visions** Level Seven by Jeanine Yeager

## Christmas stylings with a contemporary flair
## by
## Barbara Becker

**Scenes From Christmas** Intermediate Level

**More Scenes From Christmas** Late Intermediate Level